Jonathan
10. VI. 2002

Breath & Dust

Breath & Dust

Jonathan Locke Hart

[signature]

MATTOID/GRANGE

This collection published by
Mattoid/Grange
Canada, Australia, United Kingdom

Copyright © Jonathan Locke Hart 2000

ISBN 1-55195-108-8

Printed in Canada 5 4 3 2 1

Cover image: "Musing" by Jean Jackman Hart. Used by permission of the artist.

Canadian Cataloguing in Publication Data

Hart, Jonathan Locke, (date)
   Breath and dust

   Poems.
   ISBN 1-55195-108-8

   I. Title.
PS8565.A6656B72 1999   C811'.54   C99-911277-5
PR9199.3.H34877B72 1999

All rights reserved.
No part of this publication may be produced, stored in a retrieval system, or transmitted in any form or by any means—electronic, mechanical, photocopying, recording, or otherwise—without the prior permission of the copyright holder.

∞ Printed on acid-free paper.

Printed and bound in Canada by Hignell Book Printing Ltd., Winnipeg, Manitoba.

Distributed in Australia by
Mattoid
School of Literary and Communication Studies
Deakin University
Geelong, Victoria, Australia 3217

Distributed elsewhere by
The University of Alberta Press
Ring House 2
Edmonton, Alberta, Canada T6G 2E1

For MAM

Contents

Introduction   xi

I

Ancient Music	3
Buried Alive	5
The Charles	5
Bunker Hill	6
Cambridge, Mass.	6
Storrs Pond	7
River	7
The sea is calm	8
Album	8
Unburied	8
This is a land	9
Halifax	9
Ottawa	9
Orlo	10
Blue Sea Lake	10
Pointe Claire	11
Toronto	12
Lockeport	12
Not in Toronto	13
Blue Sea Lake II	13
Badlands	14
Cabin Fever	15
Fall	16
The West Bridge at Stratford	16
As the cold rain	17
Speaker's Corner	17
The Ruins at Clare	18
Girton Road	19
London Underground	20
Underground Going East	20

II

Beijing Airport Yoga	23
Stranded	23
Runway	23
Counterpoint	24
Exile	24
Scents	25
The Rain	25
Moon	25
Unquiet Thoughts	26
The Road	26
Fisherman's Song	27
Snow	27
Forest	28
Yellow River	28
Desire	28
For My Twins	29
Night Music	29
Gone	30
Arms	30
The Women	31
Rebellion	31
Night Terror	32
Solitude	32
Cold Mountain Temple	32
Flute	33
The Yangtze	33
Ruins	33
Song of Exile	34
Winter	34
Mourning	34
The Yangtze II	35
Dew	35
Women	35
Imperial Concubine	35
Morning	36
Garden Zither	36
Rain	36

Chang'an Fall	36
More Ruins	36
Lost Farms	37
To the Northern Border	37
Kept	37
Drum and Bell	37
Red Maples	38
Friends in Hong Kong	38
Lotus	38

III

Letter to India	41
Demilitarized Zone	41
Newcastle, Australia	42
Dust	42
Dog Days	43
Frost	43
The Shore	44
A Winter's Tale	44
Scars and Mirrors	44
The smell of cedar	45
The Blood-dark Sea	45
Jackhammer	46
Evening in Paris	46
Seoul National Museum	47
Why	47
When a man gets drunk	48
Dug in the bottom of my skull	49
Words	50
Signs	50
A Poet Speaks	51
No Last Word	51
A Word on Silence	52
Research	52
Chaos	53
A Satire on Myself	53
Something	54

IV

The Dead	57
Translating Antiquity	59
Reflections	59
Leaving	60
Solitude	60
My Son Asks for Love	60
Except for you	61
Dreams	61
These Words	62
If I should die	62
When the night is vacant	62
Dream Songs	63
Missing Music	63
Your fingers touched	64
The sky	64
Workhorses	64
Moon II	65
Displacement	65
Hampstead Heath	65
Monsieur Carhire	66

Introduction
by Robert Kroetsch

H ERE IS THE RESTLESSNESS of the North American poet. Jonathan Locke Hart moves us through geographies of landscape, of history, of the psyche. But this poet is unique in his resolve to find a place, not to speak about, but to speak from.

Those tentative places are as various as Ottawa and Australia, as China and a family grave. In the poem "The Charles" we read:

> The only thing real,
> He says, is the jazz of basketball,
> The choose-up game on the pavement,
> And the slow movement of a woman
> On a bicycle, asserting nothing.

The poet, finding a storied American river beside which he might speak, is displaced into a voice that flows with the river. Reading this contemporary landscape, we are reminded not only of the constant motion that constitutes our days, but also of Heraclitus.

Jonathan Hart, seeking so often to speak from a place, finds himself speaking again and again of water. Water becomes the sign of an abiding geography that will not remain still. Even ice announces a restlessness, as we see in the poem "Ottawa":

> A small child
> Skates in a tunnel of light
> As he leans
> On his hockey stick
> And ploughs through the slow, encrusted ice,
> His red woollen jacket crested with white
> And blue airplanes.

Ice, rain, mist, tides, puddles, piss, the oceans themselves, taunt Jonathan Hart in his contemporary quest for a place from which to begin his quest. He has studied our long tradition, from the romance and the epic to the terse elegance of Chinese poetry to the haunting presence and absence of Pound's "The river merchant's wife."

Jonathan Hart takes us to his own China in the poem "The Women":

> They come to the waters of Chang-an,
> Gold peacocks and silver unicorns
> On their silk gowns shimmer in the light
> Of late spring. Strings of pearls hug
>
> Their waists and curves.
>   But the white clover
> Grows here under the willow catkins
>
> That fall like snow...

Jonathan Locke Hart is the Canadian poet who cannot and yet must escape his own geographies. That tension gives him voice. In the careful extravagance of his images, in the explorations that become explorations of desire itself, he speaks for all of us who so desire to speak. He takes possession of our dispossession; he suggests how we might endure and even celebrate the fluidity of our lives.

I

Ancient Music

She has a different sense of time
And lies somewhere on the other side
Of the grave and the Atlantic, her parents
Buried in Somerset and she in Massachusetts,
And I, here, looking over a green lake
In the Rockies, think of Sarah Norton,
Centuries after.

There are doorways to the yard
I may never enter: roses are like echoes.
My dreams move over the dead leaves
And hers skirt in the dark, whisper
Over the pond in a day too long
For the two of us.

Like music
So are we. He hangs on the tree
For us both. The scars will bleed
For ever. The stars are not
Interested in algebra: freedom
Cannot be found in emblem books.
Our bodies break in the dust
We choke on, strangers of the same
Flesh.

Stillness is our family ground,
Like any other. Stone and soil
Will eat our bones even in the movement
Of desire we call voice and blood,
Quickness of tongue and eye. I
Will not bury you again
With doctrine: the red, white, yellow
Flowers blow their scent over the cape
In the heat of summer. You felt that
Too, but never in the same summer.

I would trade paradox to sit by you
To hear all those things that will erupt
Unspoken and invisible in me and mine
Without sufficient history, unconscious
As the loss we suffer, the mute sound
Of our blood inventing the past
With blind abandon. How did your head
Tilt in the wind and were you taught so well

That we speak the lesson we oppose
In time?

Perhaps it's time to read philosophy
By a dim light, to mistake a hollow rote
For stillness, to take faith for a beech tree
And leave the sand on either coast
For an urn. Our souls are blown out
On a cold wind. Perhaps this empire is
At an end even as we dissent from it
Over time.

We have our family secrets.
Multiplication is what smothers and frees us
From the rights and wrongs of forebears:
Your tears and words are swept along
And even if we could reverse the clock
The room would be too full of us
For us to talk. I have counted
Backwards to no account. See how Tom
And the schools where your brothers and father
Played with sound must be called
Back to your eyes and the sea.

We might meet at the centre of stillness
But not with incantation: we once drank beer
At Christmas and shook with laughter
Though they would make us grim
And move us to an unmoving realm.
But the sun breaks on your memory,
And in the waste I realize that, odd
As this conversation has been,
The modern world for ever young,
We are before and after
Unspoken and unseen
And love in a fiction
Whose grounds are nothing less
Than biology, as strange
And dangerous as that may seem.

Buried Alive

    We were strewn across the sea,
    Over these rocks: even now laughter
    Evaporates in a stone dew;
    The shore crumbles this tongue
    And fame fades before the beating waves.

    The Atlantic has swallowed us
    Our voices
    Lost in the roar,
    In harvest
    And burial. Salt is a taste of the fading
    Music when all else
    Sleeps.

The Charles

        The only thing real,
    He says, is the jazz of basketball,
    The choose-up game on the pavement,
    And the slow movement of a woman
    On a bicycle, asserting nothing.

        But always we return
    To the mirror and the testament, books
    About books, the self-congratulation
    Of critical discourse, finding
    Ourselves in smoke.

Bunker Hill

Somehow being near Bunker Hill,
I feel like Uranus or Lear,
The prodigal father returned
By the stealth of time: the king
Is dead, his body cast
And strewn – lye eats
And excoriates the bones of Osiris
But in the sun and celebration
Perplexed I dance inwardly
And want to be here and now.

Cambridge, Mass.

They promised it would rival
Handel's water pageant.
                         The water
Was calm and mountain-dark.
                                Police boats
Slid on their bellies like mallards.
                                    I expected
Father Thames to rise out of the weeds
And embrace his prodigal son,
But mythology grew obstinate, my knees
Sore.
        The land chills but will sweat in the morning.

Storrs Pond

In the sway of hip,
The turn of head, the wind
Skipping on the pond, the leafy
Greenness lush against the grey
Sky, he feels young again,
These men and women almost
Sway to the body.

                But if
You stop; you can hear them
Talk about ideas like a rush of geese
And if you watch, you can see
Some bodies too long at the desk.

                              The raft
Bobs in the splash and the glad roar
Under the roof carries across the water,
Here in the mountains, and the markers
Seem as strange as any boundary
Made for these souls
Halfway along the road.

River

              The trees in Cambridge
Are still umbrella-full. They wag
Like insolence in the wind.

The Charles shakes like an argument.

The women in the park sing
With lungs thrilling.

The sea is calm

The sea is calm
While thoughts of winter
Stammer from this mind
In the summer wind.

                       The silent
Moment does the most
Violence, taking us beyond
The excuse of noise.

Album

We face it
Like the last light
Where we cannot tell

Shadow from shadow.

Unburied

It seemed like home. I thought
I had read romances too long.

I am just one of many
To come from this man
Who hammered Scotland and Wales
All those centuries ago.

                       Now
I search for prairie fire.

The fields of France
From where we came
Fade,
      and time leaves us

Dead against the stars.

This is a land

This is a land stitched by distances
Where families scatter on the wind
A land rough as her
Mountains.

Here skin chaffs in the fingers
Of January.

Halifax

The hill above the harbour is immense
To a small boy.
                  The dark three storey house
Casts a long shadow.

                  Not yet three he asks his mother,
'Am I to die?' and, hurt, as if it were her fault,
She hestitates and replies, 'The doctors
Are working on it'.

Ottawa

          A small child
Skates in a tunnel of light
As he leans
On his hockey stick
And ploughs through the slow, encrusted ice,
His red woollen jacket crested with white
And blue airplanes.

Orlo

Father, mother and child sit mid-lake
In a rowboat, water calm, sky clear,
Sun hot.

           The boat, a water-spider,
Slips slowly as the three
Talk over the tranquillity.

Blue Sea Lake

All is there, mists old men rising from the lake,
Muttering loons who tuck their heads
To the untouched body of dream:
                                between
This silence the railway winds, two lines
Never touching.
                  The surface of the rails
Glows in the redness of the sun – the water
Is a dark glass, deep, long-carved by glaciers,
And no wind.

           A young boy walks with his dog,
Looks at the jointless rail bending
Around the bay to the copper rock cliff –
Shrill bird chorus breaks the still moment –
The boy sighs.
            Just as he is becoming
Gravel and water, the wind and sunlight climbing,
The dog starts, and the boy stumbles on the tie
And cries at the bruise of wonder.

Pointe Claire

A dawn so cold
The tongue rivets to steel and the youth
Trudges the snow-packed street towards the rink:
The snow on the ice rises to the ankle.

He balances on one foot
The sweat on his sock freezes in the wind
He limps like a bleeding paw.

Skate-cut, wood-knock echo
As he strides towards the net and is,
For a moment, wind

But he has to circle back: the puck
Is caught in drifting snow.

The houses, frosty and unlit,
Sit far apart, icicles
Streaming, his throat
Raw.

I come to a field:
              a blond boy
Runs, pushes
The muscles of time through
The August air:
              young deer
Sweats away the last lustre of dusk.

Their lips burn, the guilty warmth of bodies
Till the summer comes.
                        She is small and fiery as Ireland
Her tears fall on her black blouse as they stand
On the hill:
           jeering boys call from the passing car.

Time teaches him nothing
                    he is a vowel of music
Looking for a rest
                unable to measure
His breath.

He hurts her half-knowingly.
That started it all, or seemed to,
And August came once more in search
Of Fall.

Ten years have gone, and sun, snow, fence
Have no bone or blood of their own.

In the season of my exile, here down the road,
Removed I speak
To you who have never been
There.

Toronto

At the desk I look at the copper-screened picture
my brother took, the one that would capture
the last century when all film
was a red clay.
              On the station platform a dog
stands in simulacrum and in the glass
my grandfather, who knew the vast spine
of this continent, sits at his desk
writing.
        What vanishes with the dusk?

Lockeport

The old Locke houses squat on the arm,
The centuries of captains, merchants, senators
Gone.
      No more the horse
Racing on the white sweeping beach
No more the fragments of Latin and Greek,
No more the cold green of the Autumn Atlantic:

All winter now, the wooden houses
Lose to Great Lake brick.

Not in Toronto

Under wind-gusted cattails
He looks for a landscape
He seeks his mark on a rock
And listens to the wind.

There by the midnight window
His voice a vessel in a dark wood
The white caps
Crashing cymbals

Between rail and mountain
He cannot point to himself.

Blue Sea Lake II

I have lost all remembrance:
Jack-pine, chokecherry, birch,
The sun pounding the dirt road,
Lake water clean enough to drink,
The raft we dived from, clapboard
Boat-houses in a row, sunfish
Hooked and thrown back, storms
Whipping hail, beating the lake
Surface, the smell of grass
After the rain, children roasting
Marshmallows at night, the groan
Of motors, the bend of track,
Cottages built on water, dogs
Bounding after sticks, diving under
Water – nothing holding
The glasses of memory sharded,
The ears swelling with a touch
Of wind, tears
Running backwards, laughter returning
To the lungs.
           No one promised me
The world, but I expected it
Anyway.

Badlands

With certain friends we throw
off what we are, list in the dark,
eat with shadows all around, burn
our lungs with secrets in a smoke
from no convenient hell.

                                  The pain
is a bat hitting out
from the skull, this mouth
arid as the badlands, this heart
tripping in drink.

                           This is the terror,
for me now seldom, that comes
each time we talk, the wind like
the fire we breathe.

Cabin Fever

The winter in this country
Is not voluptuary
The wind passes
For dry ice.

Even the dead
Are cold here.
                The ash
On his chin burns
From within, catches a gust

And is gone.
                The sparrow
Is frozen to the window
And the dark afternoons
Close in like a vice.

No one dances in the streets
When breath freezes, when the river
Is stacked and heaving
With broken ice.

Fire, roses – imported signs –
Reduce the sentence, deflect
Defy:
          would that I were young
Again and in your arms.

Fall

They have come here
With downward looks,

Their socks are promises
And their scarves flags.

And winter will come. It always does.

No corner can shelter those who wander
The streets in winter.
                        The ghost
Of Franklin haunts these cities:
Saint Denis, Spadina, Jasper are tundra –

I cannot deny these faces.

The West Bridge at Stratford

Silence: the descending sun
Burnishes the water, the ducks
Rest their heads in wakeless reeds,
Their necks long grass
Blown over their backs as they preen,
Their eyes blinking slowly, slow
As time long before the machine clock striking,
Slow as the old monastic bell.

Bird song
Sharply sweeps the damp fields,
A poet once sat near here
And sang to the wind.

The man with the dog walks by,
Says, 'Good evening' to my 'Good day',
I was always a bit slow,
And the ducks slumber because the dog does not
See them: all is the slowly moving glass.

As the cold rain

    As the cold rain mizzles and the swish

    Of tires brushes on the distant street,
    The night
    Lies like silent dust scattered
    On my sleeve.
                I want to make this vacant
    Place a round, plump fruit,
    But my hands will not shape
    And my heart is
    The bruised space among
    The stars.
              The lint on my tongue
    Will not go away.
                  To face the grim
    Exile of night in day.
                    I would sweat
    Through death to know,
    But the wind and rain now lash
    And no
    Light will change the pain
    That takes after midnight
    When the world is all alone.

Speaker's Corner

    Here at this corner where speakers
    Hail and harangue
    Where the ancient city fills with the fat buzz
    Of traffic, where men once were hanged
    Before the throng, where pastures lay,
    And thick, oak forests spread
    North of Westminster, we watch
    Change like worms after
    A rain.

The Ruins at Clare

The moat by the broken wall
Was full until he died
In battle:
         the castle
Tumbled down, made

The houses in the village.

A college lies away
Where a portrait of Cornwallis hangs,
And the curious watch from the bridge
Where once the old quarters lay.

Even old ideas die –
        the rivers shift far and long
And our family scattered beyond the seas.

Girton Road

The pigeon was flailing on its back
Its head bloodied, its neck

Twisted, a scene that has made
Me sick since childhood: the raid

On peace the first death brought
A violence, too sudden, too hot,

The car long fled along Girton Road
The driver, hurrying to rid

Himself, herself, perhaps, of food or clothes
Or the world of animals he, she, loathes;

Perhaps it was a look away
That caused the talk and play

To stop: my children watch
The quivering beak – the grass licks

The bird's blood. No wonder
With such blunt plunder

Other worlds have been made to chase
The pain that children feel and taste.

London Underground

The sand and the sea are not here
The breathing oak leaves do not
Sigh here. The seed
In the deep furrows have fled.

Instead, the scars of years
Run along brick and pavement.
The oil in the puddles would be
A rainbow. The noise will not cease.

Underground Going East

He smells like piss
This man beside me

He picks up the paper,
Quiet as a monk, and reads
Something I will never see
And will never know.

Beijing Airport Yoga

This is when yoga would help
And so I dream of a beach
Where the waves lap
And the wind is cool
On the face, where the shade
Dances to it, and the young
Discover the heat of their bones.

Stranded

The war rages in the northern mountain
Passes: his tears fall like flowers
In the still pond.

                         His small children
Are far away in Fuzhou, and mine
In western Canada.

                         She will be alone
In her room, her hair damp with mist
And we shall look at the same moon
Through the window.

                         I have no rebel
Forces to contend with: he did
And was stranded.

Runway

The hyphens, the in-betweens
We neglect are the places
We live or die in.
                 If waiting
Were not enough, then the blossoms
Would fall on deaf ears
In their silence.

Counterpoint

I have found peace
And stepped over the heaps
Of garbage in the laneways
Like a barbarian after

The city has fallen. As
My gut howled and my limbs
Felt weak, I reached for signs,
For the spirit of the place.

My old friend Gui, as my children
Called him, chased away complaint,
His laughter the wind over a flower
His patience the moon in exile.

Amid the horn-howl I found calm,
In the campus garden I saw lovers
By the pond, great trees with high skirts
Where a young man read.

And I heard the poems I had read:
Close friends stay close wherever
They go, and the cicada's song
Feeds my ears with a quiet dew.

Exile

The cool rains fell off the Caspian
And the heat of allusion cooled
With Rome far off: while some yearn
To go home, a poet in Wu remains

Defiant, for he has spent the night
Listening to the rain as he drank
Wine with his friend, his heart ice
In a jade chalice.

Scents

This is a land of invisible smells
In gardens so quiet the dew sleeps
And the young wife of the Lu
Haunts my dreams to be young

And in a time before. I have not smelt
Tumeric and cannot imagine leaving her
For ten years beyond the frontier moon
As she spun under the swallows.

The Rain

She had small hands:
Her eyes dropped
At his gaze, the wind whipped
The puddles that seemed
Like lakes as he watched.

The trees shimmered green
Under a fluid glass
And she looked away
As if the sun were better off
Without a daughter.

Moon

The river glistens under the moon
Like beads of ice: who can tell
The sand from the moon? This light
Each dying generation has seen.

In each house a wanderer drifts
On the tide, in bed or away
To the wars. The geese are high
In the sky and a petal falls

Into the still pond, your trace
Swept in the spring river,
Hidden in the mist, seabound,
The dream of Europe at my back.

Unquiet Thoughts

Too many desires: the wind and rain
Lash the night. Soft limbs in dreams
Turn my conscience like a hot glass
Where the sun dances after the storm.

How many blossoms fell in the night?
The wild ache of exile breaks like a wave
Against my house, my children dim
Her burning eyes.

The Road

He is on the road again:
The frost has bitten the willow;
The wild bird cries; the mountain
Is an empty waste

Like Chang-an's courtesans,
The ones I hope he passes
In the night as he sees me in them
Or what I am not.

Fisherman's Song

On the long distance call
I speak to my wife about
Our children: my son cried
In gym class for the first time –

His pillow is in China.
My daughter learned to write
Her name in the nine days
I have been away.

We lost the house on the river:
My life is eventful when I am
Away – the fisher king has
Gone to waste, and all I want

Is to hear the fisherman's song
And to go home to the shore
Where the driftwood washes
And the moon is a flute or a zither.

Snow

The falcon's eyes melt the snow,
And the killing goes on
As it has always done:
The cries of children blow

Like dried leaves on a dirt road.

Forest

It could have been in the Rockies
Where the sun glows on the green moss
Deep in the forest:
In Wang Wei's lines the voices sang at dusk.

Yellow River

The snow is dusk on the river
And he would drink wine
To do homage to the gifts
Nature has given him.

He calls his son to roast
The goats, kill the cattle,
Pawn the furs to buy the wine
To banish sorrow, ancient and endless.

Desire

The crickets cry amid the frost:
She is dying of desire
For him in Chang-an, she has
Endless yearning

In sighs as steep
And blood as hot
The dreaming soul
                cannot
Reach the sleeping mat

Cold: dying, she, endless
Her yearning, and he
Absent as the shade of the moon
And the damp heat

That take him away.

For My Twins

The rabbit pounds elixir
On the moon, the shadow
Of mortar and pestle
On their faces.

Chang E stole some elixir
The Queen Mother gave
Her husband, Hou Yi,
And fled to the moon.

The elixir gave her
Lasting life: Hou Yi
Built a palace on the sun:
The light shines on their cup.

Chang E and Hou Yi meet
On the day your mother and I
Were married: you are the sun
And moon lighting up our faces.

Night Music

I haven't seen a jade flute
For years. My exile is never
To have a home. I have spoken
Out too much, so the cuckoo

Bids me farewell and return
As I turn again beyond western Hunan
At least as far as Yelang: perhaps
Some day I will write letters

From the Black Sea to Rome
Full of repentence for writing
About, for chasing, young girls
As if they had come from my poems.

Gone

    The yellow crane does not appear
    Anymore: the river mists
    Are not home, the skies empty
    And the sun sets on the fragrant grasses.

Arms

              Brambles and thorns
    Overgrow a thousand villages
    As sturdy women try to till the land
    And tend the children. We are

    The Qin, fierce in battle, driven like dogs.
    Better to have daughters than sons
    Sent to slaughter, their graves strewn
    With weeds, and in the dark, wet rain

    Their wailing pierces the dusk.

The Women

They come to the waters of Chang-an,
Gold peacocks and silver unicorns
On their silk gowns shimmer in the light
Of late spring. Strings of pearls hug

Their waists and curves.
                         But the white clover
Grows here under the willow catkins

That fall like snow: white on white
They embrace. The palace eunuchs
Ride up and down the road
Without stirring the dust.

Flute and drum play a wistful music
That stirs the dead. The prime minister
Looks for his cousin in love:
                         he loses

The red sash to a blue bird
As he steps through his lover's door.

Rebellion

Luoyang and Chang-an have fallen:
The emperor made his concubine's cousin
Prime Minister, so all An Lu-shan revolts
Though the trees and grasses flourish

And the white hair of the poet falls
Like snow. His poem is the letter
He writes himself in the absence
Of the one he so desires.

Night Terror

At Stone Moat they round up
The people in the night: the old man
Escapes over the wall. The officials
Threaten his wife, but she says:

'Two of my sons are dead in the wars,
And how much longer will the letters
Come from my third son? My grandson
Still sucks at his mother's breast.

Do you want all the males of this house?
Though I am old, let me cook for the troops.'
In the morning, the wind still, the only one
Left in the house is the old man.

Solitude

The floods rush north and south
Of the poet's cottage: the gulls still visit him;
He does not bother to sweep
The petals from the path.

He is expecting someone – his door
Is open – perhaps a woman,
Though he is still willing to call
To an old neighbour to come share home brew.

Cold Mountain Temple

From here the bell at midnight
Reaches the wanderer's boat:
Moon, crow, frost –my sleep grows
Troubled among the river maples.

Flute

He plays a flute: the moonlight is falling frost
They long for home: the pounding block
Is silent,
Thoughts like clouds pass across the mind.

The Yangtze

Somehow my hosts forgot
To show me the Yangtze
A river I drew in class
As a youth: now it will

Be difficult to imagine
Wang Jun's battleships sweeping
Down from Yizhou, crashing
Through ten thousand links

Of iron chain, till Jingling
Surrendered, and China
Was reunited once again
Once.

Ruins

The stone city is in ruins
The tide splashes against the walls
Of vacant houses: over the River Huai
The moon still wanders above the palisades.

Song of Exile

    That night the maples rustled in the wind
    And drink could not dispel our grief: the mist
    Rose high on the river and the moon sank
    Like our hearts. A woman played the pipa
    And soon appeared with
    A half-covered face. She played with such
    Yearning, emptying her passion, sometimes
    As rain drumming, sometimes as a soft stream.
    Then her song was a shattered silver
    Bottle or splitting silk.

                                    She told of how
    She had been a courtesan, learned
    The pipa from masters at thirteen, had men
    Fawning on her as she played until
    Her beauty faded, until, alone, now
    Far away she waits on an empty boat
    For her merchant husband to return.

                                              So
    For a moment
    The poet turned from his exile.

Winter

    Cold river in the snow
    The memory of smoke in autumn:
    The rush of spring
    We long for now.

Mourning

    I cannot bear to give your clothes
    Away, or to use the pots you
    Made: I yearn to meet you
    In my dreams: the sutras sung.

The Yangtze II

This was a river I drew on maps
As a child: now the barges
Move like furtive snakes
And the great waters are before me.

Dew

How much dew is needed to make
The elixir that would make the emperor
Immortal? The statue wept because
It could not answer.

Women

They are prizes of war, passed from pleasure
Palace to pleasure palace. The mounted
Horses along the red cliffs above the Yangtze
Threaten like burning arrows.

Imperial Concubine

She has been discarded at summer's end:
She watches the stars like lovers,
The Herdsman and the Weaver maid,
And scatters the fireflies with her silk fan.

Morning

Oak leaves strew the mountain paths,
Footprints in the frost lead to orange blossoms
That blow in the wind against the outpost walls
And the traveller thinks of home

Where the wild ducks mass along the curving shores.

Garden Zither

Life consumes us as death devours us:
At sunrise the poet thinks of impending night.

Rain

When will we sit by the window at home
And talk about this rain of my exile?

Chang'an Fall

On the balustrade a figure leans
Into the flute: below the lotus and mums
Are brilliant purple and scarlet – one man
Fishes in the pond, another seeks office.

More Ruins

It rains steadily along the Yangtze
The birds call above the dream
Of the six dynasties: the willows
Overgrow the great Taicheng.

Lost Farms

    May the emperor some day
    Light the feasts of those
    Who must abandon farms.

To the Northern Border

    If I awaken from my dreams
    I shall never reach Liaoning.

Kept

        The maids still
  Pluck lotus on the Yue stream.

Drum and Bell

    The drum and bell no longer mark the time
    But I can still remember carrying
    My son out on the ice at Lake Louise,
    Falling through enough to clamber to shore.

    The drum and bell no longer mark the time
    But I still think of splashing with my daughter
    In Michelon Park, of sitting her on my lap
    As I sat on the sand: in new time I feel

    The mountains of Alberta
    In the hills of China.

Red Maples

The maples turn red in autumn
In the Quixia mountains
And in the Laurentians
When I was a child.

There are clay figures
At the monastery
And the four faces appear
Amid the smoke and sacred books.

Friends in Hong Kong

They treat me to delicate fruits, and one
Is the sweetest of all, its juices dripping:
They tell me that Yang gui-fei used to send
Horsemen in relay to bring her this fruit

All the way from Canton to Chang'an:
Sometimes the horsemen died.

Lotus

In another life I might have seen her
By the imperial gate, watched the emperor
Weep as they led her before him,
Imagined that the flowers withered

As he spilt her blood after years
Of such passion. Sometimes I think I see her
In the airport, though I did not know her
Before I read of her in Nanjing

Unless I had forgotten, unless in the dream
Of heaven we shall meet, in another form,
Not in the matter of reincarnation, but
In a poem where the dew drips from a flower.

Letter to India

When the clatter is over and the stench
Of death is far, the monsoons
A memory, the dust sucked
Deep in your nostrils, think of me
And toast the death of empires.

When the signs point to desire
Beyond the northern mountains
And the high, dry air, see my face,
If you will, in the lake, and laugh.

Friend, from dark to dark, we melt
Like exhalation, we end before
We start in dreams like sweating cotton,
Afraid and happy the art we chase
Will last, in hope at least, and the cool
Drink will waste this torrid Indian feast.

Demilitarized Zone

To live an hour south
Of no man's land, to hear
The boots and tanks
From forty years ago

Perhaps in a dream
Perhaps not, is nothing
Short of unnerving, even when
She forgets and listens to the wind.

Newcastle, Australia

The sun casts: the surf turns
Beneath the blue, the birds squawk and honk
In the bush, the need for fiction being
Less here, perhaps, as no snow ever falls
And the sun burns up sin as if
It never were. For a moment
The smell of sulphur, the smoking stacks
Are forgotten, experience left
For songs the shadows sweep, the blue and gold
Are not epigrams
The wind almost seems to blow off death
Over the Pacific.

Dust

The wind scatters the frost like ashes:
Thorns tear, spears break, blood
Burning.
The crust of snow cracks,
The salts of marble selfhood
And the beasts cry under the broken skin.

The furnace stars outreach the overshot
Of the blistering sun.
                          The waters resusitate
The cool clay: the worm ropes in the dust.

And who shall answer me?

Dog Days

    August: a dog lies wheezing
    On a rancid towel,
                  I uncollar him
    Amid the slobber.

    I would be nothing
    But cartilege between your fingers –
    My bones are not sand:
    Darkness declares nothing.

    The sun burns on the water, now pales
    And skips molten gold, salmon dancing
    Spring air.
                But the dog longs for winter
    Its sweating tongue panting swallowed fire
    As the shadows fall across our faces.

Frost

    Dark by the frost on the window,
    The wind cutting through the yard,
    He walks to the barn, his nostrils pierced
    With the smell of hay.
                  The rows
    Of flanks and haunches jutting
    From their stalls, steam rising from
    Dung, cats chasing mice
    Strangely wild, the hot milk
    Spilling on steel and mud.
                  What will summer
    Bring but flies?
    What beauty in their dung-dance?
    Still his blood wants this rhythm.

The Shore

There by the lake
The grammar of the moon makes sense
Where hawk and owl stare.

No pastoral survives this place:
The dreams are stranded, the maps
Are lost in portage – the flies rip
The surface.

Fiction is a dream of grace and shape,
When we turn tears to voices,
That burn up like the morning rain.

A Winter's Tale

At doom, in the dark carpeted
Space between the stars, the night
A shroud, the house a shed, the wind
Razing it in years like days, we squat
By the fire, that old crackling light
From cave to den, our faces on
The glass screen door
Reflected and not, as we peer
At the soot and ember and gaze
Through another gauze beyond the outbuildings.

Scars and Mirrors

Blown on the wind like dandelion seed,
The choices I made or were made for me
Keep me moving, the trees rushing along
The track like shadows,
                      runways

Appearing from the cloud like Stonehenge
Or the Incan scars on the Andes.

The smell of cedar

The smell of cedar
                      the white rush
of water on rock
                  fall
    for ever
                    in the ledger
somewhere
            far from
                        looncry
  through
        bison herds
                    with
stone hammers
              heaped
                      in pits.

The Blood-dark Sea

The craft lurches
In squall and sea-sheer,
Rain lash, scald, freeze
Bow and forehead.
                    Shake and haul
On oar, heaving, he prays,
The dark waters smash
And into crashing memory
They plunge.

Jackhammer

I woke to the sound of the jackhammer
And when I pulled the drapes,
The birds were limp on the ledge,
The branches were sagging with the weight
Of the day and men clustered
Round the sewer, the street was a river,
No quiet, all waste, no sun.

The wind was old garlic,
The hammer shook the man, all watched
The pumping, breaking, beating, the smoke:
The men grow deaf. A great slate sun breaks
Through the cloud.

The sun is no chariot, the angels have
Left it, no more warriors mounting
The horses of day, but only the mechanical
Horses snorting through broken air.

Evening in Paris

The music plays,
The crowds on the sidewalks on a warm
Summer night by the Seine rise and fall
While glass
Breaks in darker streets, unheard echoes
Of a crystal night: the thunder is dry
Here, like theories made of prejudice,
The ones I heard at home,
Only the wine is better here.

Ecstasy seems far away
The whisper of leaves will come
And paradox will be shed
Like a garish coat, and metaphysics will slither
Down the bank: the markets will go belly up
In all the papers once more, and I will forget
To watch your eyes
And remember.

Seoul National Museum

    The Chinese scholar with the steady eyes
    Has taught me well: I liked him the first time
    I saw him in Seoul, and now in Beijing
    I consider his gaze as a way to calm
    Amid the Beijing clatter and rush to flight.

Why

  Why did I once feel
        that my flesh
              was birch?

But now my hands
      are syntax
         rough as philosophical

    distinction.
                Some days
I think I parse my parts to death
      and only imagine thunderous
              elk hooves on tundra.

    But what now?
               The waves seem
  to change
      the child I was
                love
  to a long
      irrevocable
               loss.

When a man gets drunk

When a man gets drunk,
Or not quite, and stumbles
Out of a warm, well-lit room
Into a dark night, the snow blasting
His glasses fast to his forehead,
The weather so much changed since
The party began, confiding to his friend,
Someone he hasn't known long, how he would
Act, make love making love a mystery,
Like the unseen stores under the skirt
Of the pine, is he telling the truth
Or just probing the air, thirsting
For the probability that nothing yields
A taste more enduring than a tart wine,
Or more dangerous than unregret, which,
Slowly, like snow, would smother the heart?

Dug in the bottom of my skull

Dug in the bottom of my skull,
                A mud, dark and reluctant, a lump
At then end of my spine, buries me,
                A string of stinging symbol,
Where Mr. Gardiner becomes a spade
And murder turns gunwale, belly
                A belltower, but much is a dry spew,
For the walls and seals that keep
The story out – the prison of signs
Pointing in all directions and none,
                So that all men split like spar
Thirsty for a mend, speaking
In circles to make womb, bed
Grave – thicken and amaze
With a far, dark fear dredged from the sea.
                Tongues are not branches
And speak only at angles.
                        Joy
Is the cry of cattle
In the distance.
We are a stutter of clay and wade
Without a map,
                The unsoloscious
Whimper at the break of day,
                            Dumb
As a thumb the sculptor left as he fled
On a one-way road.

Words

I can't help it:
These words must come
Snow in early morning
Against all prediction
Where we rise to find it.

Words break
From the undercrust,

Our heads are basements, our hearts
The theories we scrape from the cracks –
We are alone, choosing sides,
Children playing tag
With the universe.

Signs

Wind pulled tight as a bow, the sea scouring
The coast: he has striven
With dust itself, the silk and resin
Snatched from granite cases.

He is mungo on a beggar's back:
The urns are not tongues, the goats
On the altar are not keys
To the signs of sleep.

A Poet Speaks

He has big hands, a ruddy face
His white hair falls like grace
His wit does not waste
And still measures our comic days

In the shadow of the yard. That music,
Direct, subtle, strong, I could listen to beyond
This funeral day: he speaks,
Writes through the man, the land

And finds his range past fame,
Bears it well, when the quiet of poetry
Breaks open a violent world.

No Last Word

I will yearn beyond language
Even if you tell me the sea
Is only a word.

A Word on Silence

Plosive: the Word echoes
down and so the multitude
from all ages murmur
and sing of the water, now in one voice,
now in many, in harmony, in discord,
rejoice in the rose on the tomb,
afraid of
silence, the sepulchre of spent wind
and the loss of having nothing
more to say, will submerge the world.

The words have not saved us from ourselves. The beast
ravishes with jaws of shrapnel and colder
abstractions. What of Mozart when the flutes
grow raucous, turn into the muzzles of gutting
tanks, and the violins come unstrung,
their notes the warping warble of moaning
sirens to syncopated lights? What of
a poem now?

Research

I have sought hermeneutics in stacks
Along the marble floors, read love
Under the dim lights, paused by the gaps
Above and below, followed the lines
To entrance and exit, caught a couplet
At the bag-check where a mystic warns
Against doubt, while at the other end, I bet,
A blithe man checks spines amid patter
Of sports score.
    No more dust here than elsewhere:
Helen and Dido have come to Alexandria
And doubt tumbles in
Bars and opens the windows
Both.

Chaos

Even without dragons
The land is a burnt ruin.

Distance and the sea
Have made us.

The chaos of the fractured night
Dies in a salt wind.

Some say we can get
Beyond the inarticulate beast

The one that breaks
Our hearts and minds

From within.

A Satire on Myself

Shriven by a knife in the dye of night,
Tired as a vagrant without a roof – the vacant cast
Of midnight shelling my heart, and leaving
Me to consume myself, to die
By halves in artifact, to conjure doom
Gloating beyond the imagined trees – I
Try to mould this risible fiction
On this rack of bone, and make
Myself something.

Something

Somehow I find myself rolling out folds
Of examples like dough
As if compulsion to set up evidence
Before devouring it fed my words
To oblivion, and I
Wanted it that way.

It is time for a mirror and a harp
And woods where leaves are hands
And your eyes, so clear and dark,
Like water at midnight, lift
On the horizon.

IV

The Dead

The wind drifts through the stubble, dead
As winter husk, erases
The borders, obscures the ditches.
Her lips are stone, her brows
Are beaten by wind and sun,
The memory of rain fades like paint
Or love in the hot night of youth:

Some say
That blood seeps in the gravel.

She is hot moist wind
Over thick black earth, her limbs,
Round and heavy as ripe fruit, dripping
In the steam the men dream
On the banks of this stone creek.

The beating of oars in rhythm
As they watch burns off with the heat
Of an unspeakable desire.
                        They are caught
In the noise, the chorus of a song
That drums into skull and blood
Always to return when wanted least
Howling, punching, a wounded
Beast, confused and inarticulate.

The river is burnt,
As if demons still feasted
When the fire was out.
                        The bushes
Parch and scrawn, where children
Squat.
        This is the river
Of our tongue. The transvestites
Caress on its banks
And are gone in the night with no stars.
The dawn
Surprises the strays that lie by the wreckage
Under the bridge.
                    Their stomachs are swollen
From hunger, from hunger their eyes sunken.
      Graffiti scores brick soiled
Generations ago, and leaves

A trace:
   empires
Decay until they cannot taste
The sun.

They dream of dredging up the harbour
Down river.
    Tin, coins, the bones of slaves
Might lie below, boil to the surface.
   And the bread is like stone
When any can be found.

When she was younger
She sang in the orchards.
      Her house
Was not yet gutted with fire-bombs.

Those she fled
Killed land or child,
Made hell
Hands knives and wire
Minds empty stalls for slaughter,
Call down the casual horror, and call for a rain,
No ordinary rain.

Translating Antiquity

    Some ancient text lies scattered in the road,
    A child runs naked in the smoke,
                      the mirrors
    We use to bend the sun burn and crack
    Our flesh, gold sharp as razors
    On our necks, our faces scowling
    In a smash of metal and glass:
                      too much
    Alike to have ever won, we fade
    Like the memory of sulking Achilles.

    In the high pride of this retreating day,
    The last soldier buried, the cold lake
    Dark with sludge,
                    Pericles is translated
    As if he had been there,
    Garbage heaped to the windows, crows
    Picking and squawking, a statue without
        Limbs face down, so in our house
    We cannot embrace, the victim within us
        Hanging from the bridge.

Reflections

    Time crushes words in haste, though we would find
    Something solid in these hills, taste fire
    In these thousand lakes, our minds reflecting
    Dark glacial waters, our faces
    Moon and sun.
                  We invent and forget
    The dead, who flee
    And can and cannot sing.

Leaving

To leave my sleeping children
In a frozen night without stars
With Hagar and Ishmael parched
And wandering, the story read

Before they left for the stealth
Of night, to leave my wife,
A smile on her face as she breathes
To mist hardly a mirror, leads me

To ask why I travel:

                    reefs hide
Under the great green seas, like dreams.

Solitude

The day flies like sand along a solitary
Walk, the wind fades like voices of the old,
And autumn is swept like summer dirt
Under a winter carpet.

My Son Asks for Love

              The steam
On the river is nothing more
Than a song, theories

Chasing the desire of desire
Further down, away
From the reeds that bend
In the hot wind

On the Tiber.
            You and I
Hop over the syringes by the river

And pretend words are butterflies
Philosophers peering towards
The Mediterranean
Asking, as we do, for love.

Except for you

My heart is a rose
In the June sun, soft as
A cow's tongue, but
These past years, except
For you, it is chopped
Sausage on a block.

Ink is the sea
And tide the circulation
Of the blood, of beggars
On the pier, or the encephalitic
Selling newspapers, squinting, weighing
The breeze.

Dreams

Wind blasting
Berries all aground, your lips
Bit with their tang,
The sun plunging over
Your shoulder, still, we
Taste the winter,
Years slipping by in our sleep, hearts
Like battered apples, yet
We love.

    Our faces,
Wrung with a long darkness,
Dug with
The seasons:
      hung on a tree, we are felons,
Our dreams feeding us
Through winter.

These Words

You do not take these words
As your own, as if, I suppose,
Supposition were a shaken tree, broken,
The fruit half-eaten,
                    neither

In delight nor joy, the sky and sun
Mingling, nothing except tongue
Or finger.

If I should die

If I should die and you far away,
Wife, know that I wanted you by me,
That regret crossed my lips at the harm
I had done you, and hope, in the last moment,
Held up my heart, that time had not
Withered my love:
                    no, even here where
The earth lies broken in her course,
Where tears are like acid in the rain
And where the wind bites and the night
Turns against us, I did not lose faith,
Though I found in life no perfect end,
Here, where men walk alone
After their God.

When the night is vacant

When the night is vacant
As the space between
And I am as dumb
As fire,
I yearn for a stone
To rub in my hands
And wait for a sign.

Dream Songs

    On the road
    There is no station where we
    Can stop, only the sound of the wind
    In the trees, a faint light in
    The fog, or none at all, footsteps
    Scattering in our sleep.

                This child
    Will have memories after we have gone,
    Not necessarily of us, whatever we were,
    But taste and sense, traces, desire,
    The ever-plastic
    Songs the old sing the young,
    The wandering never done.

Missing Music

    The dying music of the night,
    Lights winking like fireflies.
                          The children
    Are all asleep on beds like sliderules,
                  sweat and heave
    In sheets like weeds
                  as if roots
    Would choke them.
                  We hear the knock of the ruined
    Trees in the gust,
                  our throats freeze,
    Our eyes look away
                  as if fallen leaves
    And the sweep of earth possess the music
    We lack.

Your fingers touched

    Your fingers touched a flesh
    I thought long dead,
    A sad and shaking space
    Time had hid.

                    The night wind
    Is her voice from the room
    Now empty.

                My throat grows dry
    And I weep
    Like a mute.

The sky

    The sky is smattered with stars,
    Rockface and scree sheer caught in the lake
    Catching the moon.
                    We are
    More than stone, here
    At the edge, far from the scorn
    Of semiotic whispers, shadows
    Of the shadows' sign, naked as scrub,
    Hanging at the precipice, tasting
    The blast – our feet unsure – but gazing
    Beyond.

Workhorses

    We are workhorses before the smash of stars,
    We slump and bulk under our load.
                          The buzz-saws
    Moan in the wood.
                  Our sweat glistens
    And soon the moon will rise
                      to goad us.

Moon II

The phases of the moon have drawn
Passion at the gambler's wheel,
The accident of months goes on
While dealers deal.

Displacement

                    I only presume,

a wound

          opened without a knife

                  I hope she speaks of love.

Hampstead Heath

The heath is luminous, the dark earth breathes
Delicate fire: hear us – we have shed our weariness.

Our minds are wind, water, wood
As much as bone and blood

Here on the heath, in the woods above
The city, ancestral London, here at last

I feel the sun in the dappled walk
Once the deep forest of our dreams.

The children dance and laugh
An old man, born a Victorian

Walks slowly down the path
The Thames winding over my shoulder.

No thrush sings here in this green retreat
And the sun is not purple

But I imagine glorious April
With this rude tongue

In each moment of wind
We are all or none.

Monsieur Carhire

These cars the garage men trade
Break the peace, worry the heart
Fallen on roads from Burgundy

To Bath, the same kind of sly deals
Made with the Indians.

                    These ragged
Wrecks might be parables

The bones

Long gone:

          I am stranded
On French soil with my family
And my foolishness:

              brakes,
Radiator, timing belt, camshaft
All gone like rusted warriors
Of Agincourt.

              My aunt lies dying

On the Isle of Wight.

The eyes and faces we knew: breath and dust.

Acknowledgements

THIS BOOK WAS A LONG TIME IN THE MAKING – it began in about 1974 – so memory has long ceased to be a gilded monument. May those people whose names should, but do not, appear here, excuse me. Once I thought of leaving my thanks to conversation and personal notes: the austerity appealed to me but not the possibility of apparent ingratitude. So here are acknowledgements that are too long but not long enough. My thanks to my family and friends; to my wife, Mary Marshall, and to our twins, Julia and James; and to those who listened and gave support and encouragement or who read among these poems: Sally Alcorn, Bert Almon, Ron Ayling, Douglas Barbour, Ted Blodgett, Mary Baine Campbell, Robertson Davies, Joanne Dempsey, Brian Edwards, Robert Finch, Robyn Gardner, Elizabeth Gray, Stratis Haviaras, Seamus Heaney, Greg Hollinshead, Joanne Kellock, Douglas LePan, Hugh MacKay, Desmond O'Grady, Donald and Cathleen Pfister, Gordon Teskey, Rudy Wiebe, Robert Wilson and others; to those who read the manuscript, as it now stands or in earlier forms: Alfred Alcorn, Di Brandt, Timothy Findley, Kristjana Gunnars, George Hart, Jean Jackman Hart, and Fred Wah; to those who arranged readings and especially to the members of Kirkland House, Harvard, and of the Deakin Literary Society in Melbourne; to friends and hosts in China, Korea, Hong Kong and Australia, such as Gui Yangqing, Fu Jun, Dong-Ho Kim, Ker-Yong Park, Q.S. Tong and Imre Salusinszky; to the editors of the *Antigonish Review*, *Grain*, *Harvard Review*, *Kirkland Review*, *Mattoid* and *Quarry* for placing my poems amongst your pages, some of which appear in this volume in like or later shapes. Thanks also to Brian Edwards and others at Mattoid who have supported my work and this book; to Carol Dragich, who designed and worked on the production of *Breath and Dust*; to Leslie Vermeer, who helped see this through; to Robert Kroetsch, who so generously provided an introduction; and to Glenn

Rollans, whose editorial eye and imaginative reading helped give the book the form in which it goes forth.

For earlier or original versions of the following poems in this volume, see "A Word on Silence," *Quarry* 32:3 (Summer 1983) 26-28; "When the night is vacant," *Quarry* 33:3 (Summer 1984) 61; "When a man gets drunk" and "Dug in the bottom of my skull," *Quarry* 35:3 (Summer 1986) 75-76; "Lost in Telling," Dream Songs" and "Letter to India," *Grain* 15:4 (Winter 1987) 30-31; "The Shore" and "The Dead," *Mattoid* 46/47 (1993), 103, 105-7; "Lotus," *Harvard Review* 6 (Spring 1994), 148; "The Prodigal Father"[here as "The Charles"], "Yellow River," "The Rain," "Exile," "Scents," "Cries and Whispers," [here as "Snow"], *Kirkland Review* 1 (May 1997): 23-26; "My Son Asks for Love," "Newcastle," "Counterpoint," "Moon," "The Road," "Forest," "A Poet Speaks," "Leaving," *Mattoid* 52/53 1998: 186, 188-93.